Marius von

The Stone

translated by Maja Zade

Methuen Drama

Published by Methuen Drama 2009

1 3 5 7 9 10 8 6 4 2

Methuen Drama
A & C Black Publishers Limited
36 Soho Square
London W1D 3QY
www.methuendrama.com

ISBN 978 1 408 11514 5

A CIP catalogue record for this book is available from
the British Library

Typeset by Country Setting, Kingsdown, Kent
Printed and bound in Great Britain by
CPI Cox and Wyman, Reading, Berkshire

Caution

ROYAL COURT

The Royal Court Theatre presents

THE STONE

by **Marius von Mayenburg**

translated by **Maja Zade**

First performance at the Royal Court Jerwood Theatre Downstairs,
Sloane Square, London, on 5 February 2009

THE STONE is presented as part of International Playwrights: A Genesis Project
with additional support from the Goethe-Institut London

Genesis
FOUNDATION

International Playwrights:
A Genesis Project

ROYAL COURT

off the wall
a season of new plays about germany

60 years since the foundation of the Federal Republic and 20 years
after the fall of the Berlin Wall, the Royal Court presents a season
of new plays about Germany.

25 February – 21 March

over there
By Mark Ravenhill

Harry and Luke Treadaway play twins
separated by the Berlin Wall.

A co-production with the Schaubühne am
Lehniner Platz, Berlin, supported by the
German Federal Cultural Foundation

readings of new plays from germany today

Wed 11 February, 5pm
The Final Fire (Das letzte Feuer)
by **Dea Loher**
translated by **David Tushingham**
Directed by **Hettie Macdonald**

Wed 18 February, 5pm
Black Beast Sorrow
(Schwarzes Tier Traurigkeit)
by **Anja Hilling** translated by **Philip Thorne**
Directed by **Mark Ravenhill**

Wed 4 March, 5pm
To the South Seas by Gherkin Plane
(Mit dem Gurkenflieger in die Südsee)
by **Christoph Nussbaumeder**
translated by **Meredith Oakes**
Directed by **Ramin Gray**

Wed 11 March, 5pm
The Uncertainty Of The Situation
(Die Unsicherheit der Sachlage)
by **Philipp Löhle**
translated by **Rachael McGill**
Directed by **Lyndsey Turner**

Wed 18 March, 5pm
The Pigeons (Die Tauben)
by **David Gieselmann**
translated by **Maja Zade**

Readings £8 (£6 concessions)

Over There £12 £18 £25 (Mondays all seats £10)

020 7565 5000
www.royalcourttheatre.com

International
Playwrights:
A Genesis Project

In association with
the Goethe-Institut

ARTS COUNCIL
ENGLAND

THE STONE

by **Marius von Mayenburg**

translated by **Maja Zade**

Cast in order of appearance

Hannah **Loo Brealey**
Heidrun **Helen Schlesinger**
Witha **Linda Bassett**
Mieze **Justine Mitchell**
Stefanie **Amanda Drew**
Wolfgang **Jonathan Cullen**

Director **Ramin Gray**
Designer **Johannes Schütz**
Lighting Designer **Matt Drury**
Sound Designer **David McSeveney**
Assistant Director **Lydia Ziemke**
Casting Director **Amy Ball**
Production Manager **Paul Handley**
Stage Manager **Bryan Paterson**
Deputy Stage Manager **Sarah Tryfan**
Assistant Stage Manager **Samantha Tooby**
Costume Supervisor **Iona Kenrick**
Set built by **Miraculous Engineering**

This English Stage Company's licence to present
Marius von Mayenburg's play THE STONE
in Maja Zade's translation is granted by arrangement
with Rosica Colin Limited, London, acting for
Henschel SCHAUSPIEL Theaterverlag, Berlin

THE STONE was first produced at the
Salzburger Festspiele, in a co-production with
Schaubühne am Lehniner Platz Berlin,
directed by Ingo Berk, 31 July 2008

THE COMPANY

MARIUS VON MAYENBURG (writer)

FOR THE ROYAL COURT: The Ugly One, Fireface.

OTHER THEATRE INCLUDES: Feuergesicht (Fireface), Parasiten (Parasites), Haarman, Das kalte Kind (The Cold Child), Eldorado/Turista/Augenlicht (Eyesight), Der Hässliche (The Ugly One), Freie Sicht (Moving Target), Der Hund, die Nacht und das Messer (The Dog, the Night and the Knife).

AWARDS INCLUDE: Kleist-Förderpreis für junge Dramatik for Fireface, 1997; Preis der Frankfurter Autorenstiftung during the Heidelberger Stückemarkt, 1998.

Marius took part in the Royal Court's International Residency in 1998.

LINDA BASSETT (Witha)

FOR THE ROYAL COURT: Lucky Dog, Far Away (& Albery), The Recruiting Officer, Our Country's Good, Serious Money (& Wyndhams & Public Theatre, New York), Aunt Dan & Lemon, Abel's Sister, Fen (with Joint Stock/Public Theatre, New York).

OTHER THEATRE INCLUDES: A Winter's Tale, Pericles, Henry IV Part I & II, The Theban Plays, Artists & Admirers (RSC); Phaedra (Donmar); Hortensia & The Museum of Dreams (Finborough); Love Me Tonight, Out in the Open, The Awakening (Hampstead); Richard III, Taming of the Shrew (Globe) John Gabriel Borkman (English Touring Co); Five Kinds of Silence (Lyric Hammersmith); The Triumph of Love (Almeida/UK Tour); East Is East (Birmingham Rep/ Ambassadors Theatre/Theatre Royal Stratford E/Duke of York's); The Clearing (Bush); Schism in England, Juno & The Paycock, A Place with the Pigs (National); The Seagull (Liverpool Playhouse) Medea, The Bald Prima Donna (Leicester Haymarket/Liverpool Playhouse/Almeida); George Dandin, The Cherry Orchard (Leicester Haymarket); Falkland Sound (Belgrade, Coventry).

TV INCLUDES: Larkrise to Candleford, Sense & Sensibility, The Brief, This Little Life, Our Mutual Friend, Far from the Madding Crowd, Silent Film, Christmas, A Small Dance, No Bananas, Newshounds, Bramwell, Loved Up, Skallagrig.

FILM INCLUDES: Cass, The Reader, Kinky Boots, Separate Lies, Spivs, Calendar Girls, The Last Time, The Hours, The Martins, East is East, Beautiful People, Oscar &Lucinda, Mary Reilly, Waiting for the Moon, Indian Summer.

AWARDS INCLUDE: 2004 TMA Best Actress Award for Lucky Dog, Best Actress Award Semana Internacional de Cine Valladolid Espania for East is East.

LOO BREALEY (Hannah)

FOR THE ROYAL COURT: Sliding with Suzanne.

OTHER THEATRE INCLUDES: Pornography (Traverse/Birmingham Rep); Uncle Vanya (English Touring Theatre); Little Nell (Theatre Royal Bath); After the End (Paines Plough/ Brits Off Broadway); Arcadia (Bristol Old Vic/Birmingham Rep).

TELEVISION INCLUDES: Sherlock: A Study in Pink, Hotel Babylon, Green, Mayo, Bleak House, Casualty.

RADIO INCLUDES: Nine Days Queen, The Ring and the Book, Have Your Cake, I Will Tell.

JONATHAN CULLEN (Wolfgang)

FOR THE ROYAL COURT: Talking to Terrorists, Nightsongs, Under the Blue Sky, Our Late Night, Rafts & Dreams, Gibraltar Straight, Falkland Sound, The Walldog.

OTHER THEATRE INCLUDES: State of Emergency (Gate); Happy Now?, Market Boy, Albert Speer, Ghetto, Bartholomew Fair, Fuente Ovejuna, The Strangeness of Others (National); Equus (Gielgud); The Permanent Way (Australian Tour); Master & Margerita, Nathan the Wise, The Seagull (Chichester Festival); Goodbye Gilbert Harding (Theatre Royal Plymouth); Feelgood (Garrick); Our Country's Good (Young Vic); Grace Note (Old Vic); The Merchant of Venice (Sheffield Crucible); Desire Under the Elms (Shared Experience); Vieux Carré (Nottingham Playhouse) Morning & Evening (Hampstead); The Clandestine Marriage (Queen's Theatre); Miss Julie (Salisbury Playhouse); Venice Preserved (Manchester Royal Exchange); Dr Faustus (Greenwich Theatre); Chatsky (Almeida), 'Tis Pity She's A Whore, Woman Kill'd with Kindness (RSC); Widower's Houses (Palace, Watford).

TELEVISION INCLUDES: Ghostboat, Poppy Shakespeare, Walter's War, Outnumbered.

FILM INCLUDES: Fred Claus, Finding Neverland.

AMANDA DREW (Stefanie)

FOR THE ROYAL COURT: Faces in the Crowd, The Ugly One, Mr Kolpert, The Man of Mode (& Out of Joint), The Libertine (& Out of Joint).

OTHER THEATRE INCLUDES: Parlour Song, Chain Play, Enemies, Dona Rosita the Spinster (Almeida); Otherwise Engaged (Criterion); Play (BAC); Blithe Spirit (Theatre Royal Bath/West End); Damages (Bush); 100 (The Imaginary Body); Madame Bovary, The House of Bernarda Alba (Shared Experience); Eastwood Ho!, The Malcontent, The Roman Actor (RSC/West End); The Memory of Water, Jubilee, Love in a Wood (RSC); Top Girls (New Vic); The School of Night (Minerva); Pericles (RNTS); Taking Sides (Manchester Library); John Gabriel Borkman, The Way of the World, Hove (National); The Good Times are Coming (Old Red Lion).

TELEVISION INCLUDES: Holby Blue, Eastenders, Golden Hour, The Bill, No Angels, MIT, Men Behaving Badly, Tough Love, Paul Calfes Video Diary, Soldier Soldier, Between the Lines, Full Stretch, Degrees of Error, The Maitlands.

FILM INCLUDES: The Other Man.

AWARDS INCLUDE: 2003 Clarence Derwent Award for Eastward Ho!.

MATT DRURY (Lighting)

FOR THE ROYAL COURT: Birth of a Nation, The Mother.

OTHER THEATRE INCLUDES: Private Lives, Same Time Next Year, Absent Friends, Absurd Person Singular, Deadly Nightcap, Bedroom Farce, Sweet Revenge, Joking Apart, Dead Certain, Cinderella, Dangerous Obsession, Spider's Web (Theatre Royal Windsor); Under Their Hats, (Thorndike Theatre, Leatherhead & West End), Nicholas Nickleby, The Hollow Crown, Guys and Dolls, (Thorndike Theatre, Leatherhead); The Flipside, Shirley Valentine, The Gentle Hook (Bill Kenwright); Fools Rush In (UK Tour); Funny Money (UK Tour); Two of A Kind (UK Tour); Catch Me if You Can (UK Tour); Framed (National); Cassie (Everyman, Cheltenham); Scooping the Pot (UK Tour); Daemons (European Tour); The Hollow (UK Tour), The Unexpected Guest (UK Tour); The Haunted Hotel (UK Tour); Arsenic and Old Lace (UK Tour); An Ideal Husband (UK Tour).

Matt is Head of Lighting at the Royal Court.

RAMIN GRAY (Director)

FOR THE ROYAL COURT: The Arsonists, The Ugly One, Scenes from the Back of Beyond, Woman and Scarecrow, Motortown (& Wiener Festwochen), Way to Heaven, Bear Hug, The Weather, Ladybird, Advice to Iraqi Women, Terrorism, Night Owls, Just a Bloke, Push Up, How I Ate a Dog.

OTHER THEATRE INCLUDES: Harper Regan (Salzburger Festspiele/Deutsche Schauspielhaus, Hamburg); I'll Be the Devil (RSC/Tricycle); On the Shore of the Wide World (Volkstheater, Wien); King of Hearts (Hampstead/Out of Joint); The American Pilot (RSC); The Child, The Invisible Woman (Gate); Cat and Mouse (Sheep) (Théâtre National de l'Odéon, Paris/Gate); A Message for the Broken-Hearted (Liverpool Playhouse/BAC); At Fifty She Discovered the Sea, Harry's Bag, Pig's Ear, A View from the Bridge (Liverpool Playhouse).

OPERA INCLUDES: Death in Venice (Staatsoper Hamburg/Theater an der Wien).

Ramin is an Associate Director of the Royal Court.

DAVID McSEVENEY (Sound Designer)

FOR THE ROYAL COURT: The Girlfriend Experience (& Theatre Royal Plymouth), Contractions, Fear & Misery/War & Peace.

OTHER THEATRE INCLUDES: Gaslight (Old Vic); Charley's Aunt, An Hour and a Half Late (Theatre Royal Bath); A Passage to India, After Mrs Rochester, Madame Bovary (Shared Experience); Men Should Weep, Rookery Nook (Oxford Stage Company); Othello (Southwark Playhouse).

AS ASSISTANT DESIGNER: The Permanent Way (Out of Joint); My Brilliant Divorce, Auntie and Me (West End); Accidental Death of an Anarchist (Donmar).

ORIGINAL MUSIC: The BFG (Secret Theatre Productions).

David is Sound Deputy at the Royal Court.

JUSTINE MITCHELL (Mieze)

THEATRE INCLUDES: The Hour We Knew Nothing of Each Other, Philistines, The Coram Boy, The House of Bernarda Alba, The Night Season (National); Twelfth Night (RSC); Hedda Gabler, Footfalls, Pride & Prejudice, Blythe Spirit, Bash (Gate, Dublin); Three Sisters, Aristocrats, The Shape of Metal, She Stoops to Conquer, The House of Bernarda Alba, All My Sons (Abbey, Dublin); The Way of All Fish (Bewleys, Dublin); A Midsummer Night's Dream, Dear Brutus (Nottingham Playhouse); A Streetcar Named Desire, The Importance of Being Earnest, Hayfever, A Voyage Round My Father (Pitlochry Rep); A Christmas Carol (Communicado); The Misanthrope (Borderline).

TELEVISION INCLUDES: Your Bad Self, Sleep with Me, Waking the Dead, Doctors, Afterlife, New Tricks, Joyball, The Painted Lady.

FILM INCLUDES: I Want Candy, A Cock & Bull Story, Imagine Me & You, Inside I'm Dancing, Citizen Verdict, The Honeymooners, Goldfish Memory, Conspiracy of Silence.

RADIO INCLUDES: Regenerations, Seasons of Fear.

HELEN SCHLESINGER (Heidrun)

FOR THE ROYAL COURT: Wild East, Bear Hug, The Weather.

OTHER THEATRE INCLUDES: Whipping it Up (Bush/Ambassadors); The Crucible, The Merchant of Venice, Twelfth Night (RSC); Comfort Me with Apples, No Experience Required (Hampstead); Messiah (Old Vic), Uncle Vanya, A Moon for the Misbegotten, King Lear, The Illusion, Road to Mecca (Manchester Royal Exchange); The Oresteia, War and Peace, An Inspector Calls, Inadmissible Evidence (National); An Inspector

Calls (National/Garrick); Mill on the Floss (Shared Experience); Becket (Haymarket) The Europeans (Greenwich); Tasso (Lyric Hammersmith); The Second Mrs Tanqueray, A Winter's Tale, (Salisbury); Miss Julie (Plymouth), Wild Oats (West Yorkshire); Design for Living (Harrogate); Hamlet, Romeo & Juliet (Compass Theatre).

TELEVISION INCLUDES: Trial and Retribution, Waking the Dead, Sensitive Skin, The Bill, Dirty War, Rose and Maloney, The Way We Live Now, Bad Girls, The Greatest Store in the World, Devil's Advocate, The Cormorant, Harnessing Peacocks, Bad Girl.

FILM INCLUDES: 24 Hour Party People, Persuasion.

AWARDS INCLUDE: 2006 Whatsonstage Best Supporting Actress for The Crucible; 2001 TMA Best Actress for A Moon for the Misbegotten; Best Actress Manchester Evening News Theatre Awards.

JOHANNES SCHÜTZ (Designer)

THEATRE INCLUDES (in collaboration with Jürgen Gosch): Wer hat Angst vor Virginia Woolf? (Deutsches Theater Berlin); Kätchen von Heilbronn, Bakchen (Düsseldorfer Schauspielhaus); Zurüstung für die Unsterblichkeit (Deutsches Theater Berlin); Le Maman et la Putain, Die Stunde da wir nichts voneinander wußten, Die Möwe, Endspiel (Bochum Schauspielhaus).

OTHER THEATRE INCLUDES: A Streetcar Named Desire (Theater an der Wien); Tristan und Isolde (Direction and design, Staatstheater Kassel); Antonius und Kleopatra (Bochum Schauspielhaus); Das harte Brot (Schauspielhaus Zürich); Merlin (Münchner Kammerspiele).

DANCE INCLUDES: Extensive work with Reinhild Hoffman including Erwartung/Pierrot Lunaire (Theater am Goetheplatz, Bremen); Zeche Eins (Schauspeilhaus, Bochum); Idomeneo (Direction with R. Hoffmann and stage/costume design, Oper Frankfurt).

OPERA INCLUDES: Jenufa and The Coronation of Poppea (Deutsche Oper am Rhein, Düsseldorf); Die Entführung aus dem Serail (Staatstheater Kassel); Extensive work with Peter Mussbach including Parsifal, Das Schloss (Opéra de La Monnaie, Brussels); Barber of Seville (Oper, Frankfurt)

AWARDS INCLUDE: 2007 Gold Medal Prague; 2005 Costume Designer of the Year and Quadriennale for scenography and costume for Macbeth; 2005 Stage Designer of the Year for stage design for Summerfolk.

MAJA ZADE (Translator)

TRANSLATIONS FOR THE ROYAL COURT: The Ugly One, Push Up, Fireface, Parasites, Blood.

OTHER TRANSLATIONS INCLUDE: Moving Target, God is a DJ, Eldorado, The Cold Child (from German into English); Dogville, Manderlay, Breaking the Waves, Drunk Enough to Say I Love You? (from English into German).

Maja Zade is currently dramaturg at the Schaubühne am Lehniner Platz in Berlin.

LYDIA ZIEMKE (Assistant Director)

AS DIRECTOR: The Night Before Christmas (translation and reading, Schaubühne); Stamped Oct 27th (Theatre 503); Thrown (nightmare before valentine/IUGTE International Theatre Methods Festival, Latvia); Weg-A Way (Schaubühne/Contacting the World Festival, Liverpool); Reap What You Sow (Young Vic); Leonce and Lena, Mr. Kolpert (Tabard Theatre); The Complete Truth About the Life and Death of Kurt Cobain (reading, Albany); Sunplay (reading, ET Berlin); Fireface, Pitbull, Shopping and Fucking, Like Skinnydipping (Gilded Balloon Studio Ensemble – founder and director 2001-2003).

AS ASSISTANT DIRECTOR: F.I.N.D. Festival 2006/2008, Platonov (Schaubühne, Berlin); Woyzeck (Gate); The Last Waltz Season (Arcola), La Sonnambula (Holland Park Opera), Die Mitschuldigen (Deutsches Theater, Berlin).

INTERNATIONAL PLAYWRIGHTS
AT THE ROYAL COURT

Since 1992 the Royal Court has placed a renewed emphasis on the development of international work and a creative dialogue now exists with theatre practitioners all over the world including Brazil, Cuba, France, Germany, India, Mexico, Nigeria, Palestine, Romania, Russia, Spain and Syria, and with writers from seven countries from the Near East and North Africa region. All of these development projects are supported by the Genesis Foundation and the British Council.

The Royal Court has produced new International plays through this programme since 1997, most recently *Bliss* by Olivier Choinière, translated by Caryl Churchill. In 2007, the Royal Court presented a season of five new international plays – *The Ugly One* by Marius von Mayenburg (Germany), *Kebab* by Gianina Carbunariu (Romania), *Free Outgoing* by Anupama Chandrasekhar (India), and a double bill of The *Good Family* by Joakim Prininen (Sweden) and *The Khomenko Family Chronicles* by Natalia Vorozhbit (Ukraine). Other recent work includes *On Insomnia* and *Midnight* by Edgar Chías (Mexico), *My Name is Rachel Corrie*, edited from the writings of Rachel Corrie by Alan Rickman and Katharine Viner, *Way to Heaven* by Juan Mayorga (Spain), *Amid the Clouds* by Amir Reza Koohestani (Iran), *At the Table* and *Almost Nothing* by Marcos Barbosa (Brazil), *Plasticine*, *Black Milk* and *Ladybird* by Vassily Sigarev (Russia), and *Terrorism* and *Playing the Victim* by the Presnyakov Brothers (Russia).

New German Playwrights at the Royal Court

The Royal Court began an exchange with new German playwrights in 1993 with the support of the Goethe-Institut, London. In 1994 a formal exchange continued between writers in both countries through a partnership with the Baracke of the Deutsches Theater, Berlin which later became a collaboration with the Schaubühne, Berlin.

Over the last 15 years, dozens of plays have been translated and produced as part of this long-term collaboration which has had a great impact on new writing in both countries. New German plays produced in translation at the Royal Court include: *Waiting Room Germany* (Klaus Pohl, 1995); *Strangers House* (Dea Loher, 1997); *Mr Kolpert* (David Gieselmann, 2000); *Fireface* (Marius von Mayenburg, 2000); *Push Up* (Roland Schimmelpfennig, 2002); *The Woman Before* (Roland Schimmelpfennig, 2005) and *The Ugly One* (Marius von Mayenburg, 2007 & 2008). All of this work has been supported by the Genesis Foundation and the Goethe-Institut.

The Genesis Foundation supports the Royal Court's International Playwrights Programme. To find and develop the next generation of professional playwrights, Genesis funds workshops in diverse countries as well as residencies at the Royal Court. The Foundation's involvement extends to productions and rehearsed readings. Genesis helps the Royal Court offer a springboard for young writers to greater public and critical attention. For more information, please visit www.genesisfoundation.org.uk

THE STONE is presented as part of International Playwrights, A Genesis Project, and produced by the Royal Court's International Department:

Associate Director **Elyse Dodgson**
International Administrator **Chris James**
International Assistant **William Drew**

THE ENGLISH STAGE COMPANY
AT THE ROYAL COURT

photo: Stephen Cummiskey

'For me the theatre is really a religion or way of life. You must decide what you feel the world is about and what you want to say about it, so that everything in the theatre you work in is saying the same thing ... A theatre must have a recognisable attitude. It will have one, whether you like it or not.'

George Devine, first artistic director of the English Stage Company: notes for an unwritten book.

As Britain's leading national company dedicated to new work, the Royal Court Theatre produces new plays of the highest quality, working with writers from all backgrounds, and addressing the problems and possibilities of our time.

"The Royal Court has been at the centre of British cultural life for the past 50 years, an engine room for new writing and constantly transforming the theatrical culture." Stephen Daldry

Since its foundation in 1956, the Royal Court has presented premieres by almost every leading contemporary British playwright, from John Osborne's *Look Back in Anger* to Caryl Churchill's *A Number* and Tom Stoppard's *Rock 'n' Roll*. Just some of the other writers to have chosen the Royal Court to premiere their work include Edward Albee, John Arden, Richard Bean, Samuel Beckett, Edward Bond, Jez Butterworth, Martin Crimp, Ariel Dorfman, Christopher Hampton, David Hare, Eugène Ionesco, Ann Jellicoe, Terry Johnson, Sarah Kane, David Mamet, Martin McDonagh, Conor McPherson, Joe Penhall, Mark Ravenhill, Simon Stephens, Wole Soyinka, Polly Stenham, David Storey, Debbie Tucker Green, Arnold Wesker and Roy Williams.

"It is risky to miss a production there." Financial Times

In addition to its full-scale productions, the Royal Court also facilitates international work at a grass roots level, developing exchanges which bring young writers to Britain and sending British writers, actors and directors to work with artists around the world. The research and play development arm of the Royal Court Theatre, The Studio, finds the most exciting and diverse range of new voices in the UK. The Studio runs play-writing groups including the Young Writers Programme, Critical Mass for black, Asian and minority ethnic writers and the bi-annual Young Writers Festival For further information, go to www.royalcourttheatre.com/ywp

"Yes, the Royal Court is on a roll. Yes, Dominic Cooke has just the genius and kick that this venue needs... It's fist-bitingly exciting." Independent

PROGRAMME SUPPORTERS

The Royal Court (English Stage Company Ltd) receives its principal funding from Arts Council England, London. It is also supported financially by a wide range of private companies, charitable and public bodies, and earns the remainder of its income from the box office and its own trading activities.

The Genesis Foundation supports the Royal Court's work with International Playwrights.

The Jerwood Charitable Foundation supports new plays by new playwrights through the Jerwood New Playwrights series.

The Artistic Director's Chair is supported by a lead grant from The Peter Jay Sharp Foundation, contributing to the activities of the Artistic Director's office. Over the past ten years the BBC has supported the Gerald Chapman Fund for directors.

ROYAL COURT DEVELOPMENT ADVOCATES
John Ayton
Anthony Burton
Sindy Caplan
Cas Donald
Allie Esiri
Celeste Fenichel
Stephen Marquardt
Emma Marsh (Vice Chair)
Mark Robinson
William Russell (Chair)

PUBLIC FUNDING
Arts Council England, London
British Council
London Challenge

CHARITABLE DONATIONS
American Friends of the Royal Court Theatre
Gerald Chapman Fund
Columbia Foundation
The Sidney & Elizabeth Corob Charitable Trust
Cowley Charitable Trust
The Edmond de Rothschild Foundation*
The Dorset Foundation
The D'Oyly Carte Charitable Trust
E*TRADE Financial
Esmée Fairbairn Foundation
The Edwin Fox Foundation
Francis Finlay*
The Garfield Weston Foundation
Genesis Foundation
Haberdashers' Company
Jerwood Charitable Foundation
John Thaw Foundation
Kudos Film and Televisoin
Lloyds TSB Foundation for England and Wales
Dorothy Loudon Foundation*
Lynn Foundation
John Lyon's Charity

The Laura Pels Foundation*
The Martin Bowley Charitable Trust
Paul Hamlyn Foundation
The Peggy Ramsay Foundation
Quercus Charitable Trust
Jerome Robbins Foundation*
Rose Foundation
Royal College of Psychiatrists
The Royal Victoria Hall Foundation
The Peter Jay Sharp Foundation*
Sobell Foundation
Wates Foundation

SPONSORS
BBC
Links of London
Pemberton Greenish

BUSINESS BENEFACTORS & MEMBERS
Grey London
Hugo Boss
Lazard
Merrill Lynch
Vanity Fair

INDIVIDUAL SUPPORTERS

ICE-BREAKERS
Act IV
Anonymous
Ossi & Paul Burger
Mrs Helena Butler
Cynthia Corbett
Shantelle David
Charlotte & Nick Fraser
Mark & Rebecca Goldbart
Linda Grosse
Mr & Mrs Tim Harvey-Samuel
The David Hyman Charitable Trust
David Lanch
Colette & Peter Levy
Watcyn Lewis
David Marks

Nicola McFarland
Janet & Michael Orr
Pauline Pinder
Mr & Mrs William Poeton
The Really Useful Group
Lois Sieff OBE
Gail Steele
Nick & Louise Steidl

GROUND-BREAKERS
Anonymous
Moira Andreae
Jane Attias*
Elizabeth & Adam Bandeen
Philip Blackwell
Mrs D H Brett
Sindy & Jonathan Caplan
Mr & Mrs Gavin Casey
Carole & Neville Conrad
Clyde Cooper
Andrew & Amanda Cryer
Robyn M Durie
Hugo Eddis
Mrs Margaret Exley CBE
Robert & Sarah Fairbairn
Celeste & Peter Fenichel
Andrew & Jane Fenwick
Ginny Finegold
Wendy Fisher
Hugh & Henri Fitzwilliam-Lay
Joachim Fleury
Lydia & Manfred Gorvy
Richard & Marcia Grand*
Reade and Elizabeth Griffith
Nick & Catherine Hanbury-Williams
Sam & Caroline Haubold
Mr & Mrs J Hewett
Nicholas Josefowitz
David P Kaskel & Christopher A Teano
Peter & Maria Kellner*
Mrs Joan Kingsley &
Mr Philip Kingsley
Mr & Mrs Pawel Kisielewski
Varian Ayers & Gary Knisely
Rosemary Leith
Kathryn Ludlow
Emma Marsh
Barbara Minto
Gavin & Ann Neath

William Plapinger & Cassie Murray
Mark Robinson
Paul & Jill Ruddock
William & Hilary Russell
Jenny Sheridan
Anthony Simpson & Susan Boster
Brian Smith
Carl & Martha Tack
Katherine & Michael Yates

BOUNDARY-BREAKERS
John and Annoushka Ayton
Katie Bradford
Tim Fosberry
Edna & Peter Goldstein
Sue & Don Guiney
Rosanna Laurence
The David and Elaine Potter Foundation

MOVER-SHAKERS
Anonymous
Dianne & Michael Bienes*
Lois Cox
Cas & Philip Donald
John Garfield
Duncan Matthews QC
Jan & Michael Topham

HISTORY-MAKERS
Jack & Linda Keenan*
Miles Morland
Ian & Carol Sellars

MAJOR DONORS
Daniel & Joanna Friel
Deborah & Stephen Marquardt
Lady Sainsbury of Turville
NoraLee & Jon Sedmak*

*Supporters of the American Friends of the Royal Court

FOR THE ROYAL COURT

Royal Court Theatre, Sloane Square, London SW1W 8AS
Tel: 020 7565 5050 Fax: 020 7565 5001
info@royalcourttheatre.com, www.royalcourttheatre.com

Artistic Director **Dominic Cooke**
Associate Directors **Ramin Gray*, Jeremy Herrin,
Sacha Wares+**
Artistic Associate **Emily McLaughlin**
Associate Producer **Diane Borger**
Diversity Associate **Ola Animashawun***
Education Associate **Lynne Gagliano***
Trainee Director (ITV Scheme) **Natalie Ibu‡**
Personal Assistant to the Artistic Director **Victoria Reilly**

Literary Manager **Ruth Little**
Literary Associate **Terry Johnson***
Senior Reader **Nicola Wass****
Pearson Playwright **Daniel Jackson†**
Literary Assistant **Marcelo Dos Santos**

Associate Director International **Elyse Dodgson**
International Administrator **Chris James**
International Assistant **William Drew**

Studio Administrator **Clare McQuillan**
Writers' Tutor **Leo Butler**

Casting Director **Amy Ball**
Casting Assistant **Lotte Hines**

Head of Production **Paul Handley**
JTU Production Managers **Sue Bird, Tariq Rifaat**
Production Administrator **Sarah Davies**
Head of Lighting **Matt Drury**
Lighting Deputy **Nicki Brown**
Lighting Assistants **Stephen Andrews, Katie Pitt**
Head of Stage **Steven Stickler**
Stage Deputy **Duncan Russell**
Stage Chargehand **Lee Crimmen**
Chargehand Carpenter **Richard Martin**
Head of Sound **Ian Dickinson**
Sound Deputy **David McSeveney**
Head of Costume **Iona Kenrick**
Costume Deputy **Jackie Orton**
Wardrobe Assistant **Pam Anson**
Sound Operator **Alex Caplan**

Executive Director **Kate Horton**
Head of Finance and Administration **Helen Perryer**
Planning Administrator **Davina Shah**
Senior Finance and Administration Officer **Martin Wheeler**
Finance Officer **Rachel Harrison***
Finance and Administration Assistant **Tessa Rivers**
Interim Personal Assistant to the Executive Director
Frances Marden

Head of Communications **Kym Bartlett**
Marketing Manager **Becky Wootton**
Press & Public Affairs Officer **Stephen Pidcock**
Audience Development Officer **Gemma Frayne**
Sales Manager **Kevin West**
Deputy Sales Manager **Daniel Alicandro**
Box Office Sales Assistants **Ed Fortes, Shane Hough,
Ciara O'Toole**

Head of Development **Jenny Mercer**
Senior Development Manager **Hannah Clifford**
Corporate Associate **Sarah Drake***
Development Officer **Lucy James**
Development Assistant **Penny Saward***

Theatre Manager **Bobbie Stokes**
Front of House Manager **Claire Simpson**
Deputy Theatre Manager **Daniel O'Neill**
Café Bar Managers **Paul Carstairs, Katy Mudge**
Head Chef **Stuart Jenkyn**
Bookshop Manager **Simon David**
Assistant Bookshop Manager **Edin Suljic***
Bookshop Assistant **Emily Lucienne**
Building Maintenance Administrator **Jon Hunter**
Stage Door/Reception **Simon David*, Paul Lovegrove,
Tyrone Lucas**

Thanks to all of our box office assistants, ushers and bar staff.
+ Sacha Wares' post is supported by the BBC through the Gerald Chapman
Fund.
** The post of Senior Reader is supported by NoraLee and Jon Sedmak
through the American Friends of the Royal Court Theatre.
‡ The post of Trainee Director is supported by ITV under the ITV Theatre
Director Scheme.
† This theatre has the support of the Pearson Playwrights' scheme,
sponsored by the Peggy Ramsay Foundation.
* Part-time.

ENGLISH STAGE COMPANY

President
Sir John Mortimer CBE QC

Vice President
Dame Joan Plowright CBE

Honorary Council
**Sir Richard Eyre CBE
Alan Grieve CBE
Martin Paisner CBE**

Council
Chairman **Anthony Burton**
Vice Chairman **Graham Devlin**

Members
**Jennette Arnold
Judy Daish
Sir David Green KCMG
Joyce Hytner OBE
Stephen Jeffreys
Wasfi Kani OBE
Phyllida Lloyd
James Midgley
Sophie Okonedo
Alan Rickman
Anita Scott
Katharine Viner
Stewart Wood**

The Stone

Characters

Witha
Wolfgang, *her husband*
Heidrun, *her daughter*
Hannah, *her granddaughter*
Mieze
Stefanie

1993

Witha *is sitting under the table.*

Hannah   You know.

Heidrun   What is it, Hannah?

Hannah   I don't want to be here.

Heidrun   We'll have coffee and cake in a minute.

Hannah   Every morning when I wake up I think I must
be back in my old room. I open my eyes and I get a fright.
The walls in the room are so blue in the morning. And it's so
quiet, only the leaves rustle.

Heidrun   Maybe we'll use the nice china today. What do
you think, Mother?

Witha   In the basement, it's safe.

Hannah   I shake my head so I wake up, so everything moves
into place and I'm back home, but my old room is gone, I'm
already awake, as awake as I'm going to get, no matter how
wide I open my eyes.

Heidrun   Do you want to use the nice china, Hannah?

Hannah   Are you listening to me?

Heidrun   What is it, child?

Hannah   I don't want to be here.

Heidrun   Don't you like it?

Hannah   I don't belong here.

Heidrun   Pity.

Hannah   Stop saying pity, Mum.

Heidrun   But I think it's a pity.

Hannah   It's as if you've given up on me.

Heidrun   What am I supposed to do? I think it's a pity —
such a lovely house, a lovely room, a lovely new bed and you
don't want to be here.

Hannah   As if I'm a disappointment: pity. You could make
an effort, but you won't even ask me why.

Heidrun   Because I take you seriously, because you've grown
up. I'm not going to start a discussion.

Hannah   Maybe I don't want you to take me that seriously.
Maybe I'm not that grown up yet.

Heidrun   All of a sudden.

Hannah (*to* **Witha**)   Do you want to be here?

Witha   Where?

Hannah   In this house? In this town?

Heidrun   Granny used to live in this house, of course she
wants to be here.

Witha   Where? Where do I want to be?

Hannah   Then why is she sitting under the table?

Heidrun   Mother? Why are you sitting under the table?

Hannah   She never used to do that.

Witha   Child, what are you still doing out there?

Hannah   It started when we came here.

Witha   Can't you hear the siren? You're really scaring me.

Hannah   It's because Granny is getting bombed again.

Heidrun   We're not getting bombed, Mother, on the contrary,
everything has been rebuilt.

Witha   He said if I go into the basement the whole house
will crash down.

Hannah   Doesn't look as if she wants to be here.

Witha   The siren.

1935

Mieze   We can have a chat in the meantime. Won't you have a seat, Mrs Heising?

Witha   If you don't mind.

Mieze   I don't. Make yourself at home.

Witha   Not yet.

Mieze   It won't take long. The contract is drawn up, your husband just needs to sign it, and then it's all yours. Just enough time for a coffee.

Witha   Then I'll have one.

Mieze   You'll have one?

Witha   A coffee.

Mieze   You'll take one? With both hands?

Witha   What?

Mieze   Is that your style, that you take things?

Witha   I'm afraid I don't follow. What did you say?

Mieze   Nothing. Here's your coffee. Go ahead and take it.

1993

Heidrun   Maybe your grandfather.

Hannah   I don't have a role model, why should I come up with one now? I'll go there tomorrow and say: I don't have a role model. End of presentation. As if everyone needs a role model, and Sylvia actually stood there and said, my role model is Mrs Döbner. Mrs Döbner. We couldn't even laugh at her we were so shocked, and then she said that Mrs Döbner was a good teacher and fair and funny, and that she has a lovely hairstyle, and she was completely serious. I don't have a role model. Or I can say, Sylvia is my role model because she does such lovely presentations.

Heidrun   Why not your grandfather?

Hannah   He's a man, and apart from that I don't even know him.

Heidrun   That doesn't matter.

Hannah   How can he be my role model when I don't know him?

Heidrun   Lots of people have role models they don't know. Like Napoleon.

Hannah   But my grandfather wasn't Napoleon. Napoleon is in every history book, they've named streets after him.

Heidrun   But your grandfather did things you can be proud of, more than Napoleon, who waged wars.

Hannah   Maybe I don't want to be proud.

Heidrun   Pity. Your grandfather deserves it.

Hannah (*giving her presentation*)   In my family we don't really talk about it, but my grandfather saved a Jewish family. Schwarzmann. He was my grandfather's boss at the Veterinary Institute until he was forced to resign under the Nazis. My grandfather stood by him, and in 1935 he financed his escape. The Schwarzmanns emigrated to the US via Amsterdam. Mrs Schwarzmann is still living in New York and is a well-known gallery owner and art dealer. She made Max Beckmann famous in America. My grandfather is my role model because he stood by his friends and was persecuted by the Nazis because of it.

Heidrun   Lovely.

1993

Hannah   There.

Heidrun   Where?

Hannah   There, in the garden.

Heidrun   Everything is black.

Hannah   Between the trees.

Witha   You talk too much when you're eating.

Heidrun   There's nothing there, child.

Hannah   The swing, see that?

Heidrun   That's the wind.

Hannah   See the way it's swinging?

Witha   If she talks when she's eating her teeth are going to fall out of her mouth.

Heidrun   Who's going to fall out of what?

Witha   Me? No one, I didn't say anything.

Heidrun   You were talking about your teeth again.

Witha   Mieze. If she talks when she's eating they're going to fall onto the plate.

Heidrun   And now you're going to be quiet and eat.

Witha   Yes. I saw Mieze in the street. God, she's grown old, an old woman, pushing one of those little carts with nothing inside, that's what it's like, nothing left, pushing an empty little cart, looks like a madwoman, an empty pram or something, as if you're dragging a leash behind you, without a dog.

Heidrun   Wait, Mother, I'll fix your napkin.

Witha   Myself, I'll do it myself. I'm not that old.

Hannah   There, across the lawn.

Heidrun   Child, eat or your eyes will get even bigger.

Witha   That's why I don't talk when I'm eating.

Heidrun   You're talking the whole time.

Hannah   Maybe it's Dad.

Heidrun   Who?

Hannah   Maybe he's come back.

Heidrun   I don't think that Dad is skulking round the garden.

Hannah   Maybe he's brought his spade and is digging a hole.

Heidrun   Child. I know you miss him. And I'm sure he misses you too.

Hannah   That's why he's come back.

Heidrun   He's not coming back, and if he is he'll use the doorbell.

Hannah   He's in the garden.

Heidrun   There's no one in the garden. Because we haven't let anyone in.

Hannah   Someone has climbed over the wall, pushed the swing and is now standing between the trees.

Witha   And you're much too old for the swing.

Heidrun   Shall we go and have another look at the wall? Have you forgotten about the spikes on top of the wall? How is anyone going to climb over them and not get hurt?

Hannah   Maybe he is hurt. Maybe Dad climbed over the wall and is hurt and crawling between the trees.

Heidrun   I don't want to hear anything else about Dad.

Witha   Your husband should be here at the table drinking the coffee you made. If he had even the tiniest sense of responsibility – even the tiniest – but he doesn't, because he's a whatsit – a – you know – he's a bastard.

Heidrun   No he's not.

Hannah (*to* **Witha**)   And where is your husband?

Heidrun   He just couldn't live with me any more.

Witha (*to* **Hannah**)   What, child?

Hannah   Your husband. He's not here either, is he? Doesn't he have the tiniest either? Is he a bastard as well?

Witha (*to* **Heidrun**)   What is she talking about?

Heidrun   Nothing. (*To* **Hannah**.) Quiet now.

Witha   What is your child talking about? Didn't you teach her any breeding, that she's talking like this?

Heidrun (*to* **Hannah**)   You know perfectly well that your grandfather is dead.

Hannah   But Dad isn't dead and Dad's not a bastard, it's just a difficult time right now, and he'll take me to Spain when it's all over, and I'm not meant to think it's my fault.

Heidrun   That's right, it's not your fault, it's mine.

Hannah   He said it was the house.

Witha   What house?

Hannah   The house. This house. He says Mum is married to the house and he doesn't want to – oh.

Heidrun   What?

Hannah   There. At the window.

Heidrun   Oh.

Hannah   That's not Dad.

Heidrun   No.

Witha   What?

Hannah   There, at the window.

Witha   Where?

Hannah   Someone's there.

Witha   What are you wittering on about?

Hannah   Take a look. There.

Witha   Oh.

Heidrun   Yes.

Hannah   A woman.

Stefanie   I've come to bother you.

1935

Mieze   We had the spikes put on the wall for security.

Witha   Yes.

Mieze   It would have been nicer without the spikes.

Witha   Of course.

Mieze   But the house is completely unprotected from the garden.

Witha   Did anything ever – did anyone – ?

Mieze   Did anything happen?

Witha   Did anyone get into the –

Mieze   In the winter, before the spikes went up. Two boys in uniform. I shouted from the veranda until they got scared. They threw their bags over the wall and slowly disappeared into the dark.

Witha   But since you got the spikes?

Mieze   People throw rubbish over the wall and last week a dead cat.

Witha   So it worked?

Mieze   What?

Witha   The spikes. Did the spikes work?

Mieze   Yes, sure. No. In the end. We're moving out. And you're moving in.

Witha   But that has nothing –

Mieze   You can get rid of the spikes

Witha   I'd rather not.

Mieze   Don't worry, they're not going to hurt you. You're one of them.

Witha   We're not – we're no – we've never been –

Mieze   Of course not, I didn't mean to suggest that you were. You'll have a lovely time here, that's all I meant.

Witha   Lovely.

Mieze   And we'll be – we'll be so far away that you won't ever have to think about – we'll be gone.

Witha   Are the men almost done in there?

Mieze   Would you like another coffee while we wait?

1993

Stefanie   I don't want any coffee, I'm here to bother you.

Heidrun   Who are you?

Witha   What's wrong with our coffee?

Stefanie   You know me.

Heidrun   No.

Stefanie   It's all right. Unpleasant faces are easily forgotten, and I'm sure my face is very unpleasant for you.

Heidrun   No, it means nothing to me.

Stefanie   I on the other hand never forgot your face. Your face was pleasant for me. Back then you promised me chocolate.

Witha   Would she prefer hot chocolate? (*To* **Heidrun**.) Go on, Heidi, make her a cup of cocoa.

Heidrun   I promised you – ? Your face is quite pretty, but I can't for the life of me –

Stefanie   I was younger back then.

Heidrun   When?

Stefanie (*to* **Hannah**)   Younger than you. Do you still go on the swing?

Heidrun   What do you mean – back then?

Stefanie   Already too old for the swing? How old are you? Fourteen? Fifteen?

Hannah   I thought you were my father.

Stefanie   Your mother was pregnant with you, barely made it up the stairs you were so heavy. I don't have any children.

Hannah   I still fit on the swing, I'm not heavy.

Stefanie   In which direction do you swing? Towards the forest or the house?

Heidrun   Leave the child alone.

Stefanie   Is that nice, when the forest rushes towards you?

Heidrun   Wouldn't you rather tell me what you want?

Stefanie   I already have. I'm here to bother you.

Heidrun   You succeeded, you can go now.

Stefanie   But I haven't congratulated you yet.

Heidrun   What for?

Stefanie   You moving in. Do you like it here?

1935

Witha   Yes. Of course.

Mieze   Of course. Otherwise you wouldn't –

Witha   No, I think your house is very beautiful.

Mieze   So do I.

Witha   Of course.

Mieze   It'll be yours soon.

Witha   Yes.

Mieze   If the gentlemen in there can come to an agreement. No. What I meant to say −

Witha   I particularly like the garden. That there are trees and a veranda. What kind of bushes are they, is that a rhododendron?

Mieze   What about the furniture?

Witha   What?

Mieze   In here. The furniture.

Witha   Yes. Lovely. Modern.

Mieze   Because we're not fond of dark, heavy things.

Witha   Lovely.

Mieze   But of course that's up to you. If you want to live in Gothic oak − it'll be yours. I just think the atmosphere of the house −

Witha   I completely agree.

Mieze   They're all designs from the past couple of years.

Witha   Yes. You can tell. Is that − ?

Mieze   A sideboard.

Witha   A sideboard?

Mieze   Yes.

Witha   Aha.

Mieze   Are you going to throw all it all out?

Witha   I don't know what my husband −

Mieze   Go ahead, it's not like we can take it with us.

Witha   No.

Mieze   Of course not. Just a few suitcases.

Witha   I'm sorry −

Mieze   You don't have to apologise.

Witha   I'm not apologising.

Mieze   I just wanted to know if you like it here, because it would be a shame if we move out and you don't even like it.

1993

Heidrun   No, of course, I like it.

Stefanie   Because it would be absurd if I'd had to move out and you don't even like it.

Heidrun   Why − where did you have to, when − ?

Stefanie (*to* **Hannah**)   Did you grow up here? Of course not.

Hannah   I'm not a child any more.

Stefanie   But you still go on the swing. You know who put it up?

Hannah   No, the swing was already here. My grandfather?

Stefanie   Your what?

Hannah   I said I don't know.

Stefanie   It was my grandfather. He borrowed a ladder, left in the morning, walked down the road, came back in the afternoon, the ladder over his shoulder, his shoes and trousers full of dust up to his belt, it's still the same rope, he took it to the mountains as a young man, saved his life more than once, but he cut it in two for my swing, slung the ends over the branch, high up on the ladder, lined it with a torn towel so the rope doesn't get frayed, and tied the swing board at the bottom. In which direction do you swing? Towards the forest or the house?

Hannah   Do I have to decide?

Stefanie   Towards the forest, the other children always wanted to swing towards the forest. I faced the house. My grandfather is standing behind me and catches me before he pushes me again, and then I fly up the facade, up the veranda with the large folding door, the balcony on top of the conservatory and the roof with the dark hatches and the chimney, and the sky above.

Witha   Aren't you much too old to go on the swing?

Heidrun   She lived here, apparently – apparently she used to live here.

Stefanie   For a brief moment I'm standing in the sky, my upper body falls backwards, the swing board teeters and almost tips over, then the dark grass sucks me back down, the facade races past me, I smell something like vertigo in my nose, and then my grandfather, who is standing by the maple tree and reaching out to me.

Heidrun   You used to live here.

Stefanie   Yes, you brought me chocolate. From the West. You were very nice back then.

1978

Heidrun *is pregnant.*

Heidrun   Thank you for the coffee. We brought you this.

Stefanie   Is that chocolate?

Heidrun   Yes.

Stefanie   But –

Heidrun   Go on and take it.

Stefanie   How did you know there was a child here?

Heidrun   Sometimes adults like chocolate too.

Witha   And you're not that young any more.

Stefanie   Right. I'm quite old. You probably want to see everything now.

Heidrun   Just the garden.

Stefanie   But it's a mess. My grandad is ill.

Witha   I'm sorry to hear that.

Stefanie   I'll ask him. He's seventy. I'm sure he'll be happy to see someone from the old days.

She stands up and leaves.

Heidrun (*as* **Stefanie** *is leaving*)   We just want to see the −

Stefanie *has left. Nothing*

Witha   I don't want to talk to him.

Heidrun   It's good that we know him.

Witha   What's good about it? He stole our chickens after the war.

Heidrun   Quiet. That's over twenty years ago.

Witha   And stood behind his curtain when I was on the terrace. I don't want to see him.

Heidrun   His granddaughter is nice.

Witha   Henriette and Adele.

Heidrun   Who?

Witha   The chickens. I walked all the way to Ruppendorf and bought them with the jewellery the Russians didn't find, and he stole them and ate them.

Heidrun   Quiet. They would have ended up in the soup by now anyway.

Witha   Like the soldiers, when they fall in battle.

Heidrun   Why soldiers?

Witha   Because what would have happened by now is not the point. Your father could have died of natural causes by now, nonetheless it's terrible that the Russians shot him and he barely knew you. It's not about whether you end up in the soup or not, but about how many eggs you lay before that, because that means you had a life.

1945

Wolfgang   They won't do it.

Witha   Everyone says it's going to happen. With so many refugees in town.

Wolfgang   Churchill has an aunt that lives up by the Weisser Hirsch.

Witha   Really?

Wolfgang   He's not going to bomb his own aunt.

Witha   He's not thinking about his aunt. The Albrechts have gone to Ruppendorf and they say there's plenty of room.

Wolfgang   That bad?

Witha   It provokes them that we're so beautiful. The town glitters and that's why it has to go.

Wolfgang   They hate us. They always have.

Witha   Please. I know it's going to happen.

Wolfgang   Then it really is better if you take Heidrun to the countryside. You'll have more food there, too.

Witha   And you?

Wolfgang   What about me?

Witha   I'm supposed to go by myself?

Wolfgang   I'd feel like a deserter.

Witha   You can come back when it's over.

Wolfgang   To what, if it's over? The house won't be here, and there'll be refugees in the ruins. I can't leave all this – my house, my Institute, my colleagues, my animals. Life has to carry on.

Witha   And if it doesn't?

Wolfgang   What?

Witha   If it stops? If this life is extinguished and stops?

Wolfgang   Then it stops. Then the others were more viable.

Witha   As if we're bacteria in a Petri dish.

Wolfgang   You're a mother with a child, I can understand that you're worried, but as a man I have duties that go beyond.

Witha   It's not about the child. It's you I'm worried about.

Wolfgang   Me?

Witha   You keep talking about the end, sometimes I think you're toying with the idea.

Wolfgang   Because then you'd be left alone with the child?

Witha   You keep talking about the child as if all I am is a mother. Forget about the child, I could never be happy again.

Wolfgang   That's nice of you.

Witha   No, stupid. It's stupid of me. To cling to such a stubborn man.

Wolfgang   Who else would you cling to?

Witha   So I'll stay here, and if we kick the bucket the others were viable and we weren't.

1953

Witha *is sorting through letters stored in a shoebox.*

Heidrun   Are you crying?

Witha   I can't take them with me. Not all of them.

Heidrun   Are they from Father?

Witha   Or they'll know at the border that we're not coming back.

Heidrun   Can I have a look?

Witha   Love letters.

Heidrun   Sorry.

Witha   No. Go ahead. They're beautiful. You should look at your father's handwriting.

Heidrun   Now?

Witha   Tomorrow we'll be gone, and I can only take two or three.

Heidrun   And the others?

Witha   I have to put them away.

Heidrun   Which ones? Which ones are you going to put away?

She takes a letter from the box, looks at it.

Witha   Or they'll read them when they tear everything apart here.

Heidrun   His writing is like mine. How are you going to decide?

She takes a stack from the box. Something small falls out from between the letters. She picks it up.

And this?

Witha   What is it?

Heidrun *holds it up so she can see it.*

Heidrun   There's a swastika attached to it.

Witha   Was that in there?

Heidrun   What is it?

Witha   People used to put it on their coats.

Heidrun   Who?

Witha   If you were a Party member.

Heidrun   But Father wasn't a Party member.

Witha   No.

Heidrun   Or was Father a Party member?

Witha   No.

Heidrun   Father hated them. They threw stones at him, he wasn't in the Party.

Witha   Exactly. It's not his.

Heidrun   But what is it doing in his box?

Witha   It's not his box. It's my box. He sent the letters to me, and I kept them. In my box.

Heidrun   I don't understand.

Witha   It's my badge. I thought I buried it in the garden when the war ended. I don't know how it got in there.

Heidrun   Your badge.

Witha   Yes.

Heidrun   But you weren't in the Party.

Witha   Look. It's not as if you were always able to do what you wanted.

Heidrun   You hated them, they threw stones at him.

Witha   But I still had to join the Party. Black hair, and the shape of my face – they spat at me in the tram and tried to throw me out of the carriage.

Heidrun   Did they throw you out?

Witha   I had the badge. Lots of people did it.

Heidrun   Your face?

Witha   I can understand that you're confused, but why would I lie to you? You're old enough.

Heidrun   I'm not confused.

Witha   We'll bury it in the garden.

Heidrun   Together with the letters?

Witha   If you want we'll dig a second hole.

Heidrun   Yes.

Witha   You don't have to look at me like that.

Heidrun   I can't believe that Father went along with it.

Witha   Your father was not a hero, but he always resisted. Not for political reasons, but as a matter of principle. If someone said something, he was against it because he wanted to know if there was something behind it. Of course a lot of things got broken, but a frog breaks if you dissect his nerves, and that's what he was, a veterinarian, a man of science.

1935

Wolfgang   Are you happy, Witha?

Witha   We're here now.

Wolfgang   What are we going to do with this awful furniture?

Witha   Some of it isn't so bad, and we'll sell the rest.

Wolfgang   As if we're moving into someone else's life.

Witha   Isn't it for the best? They wouldn't have been able to stay here. Look at the rhododendron, it's in bloom.

Wolfgang   It doesn't notice a thing.

Witha   What should it notice?

Wolfgang   Nothing. It's just one of those moments.

Witha   Since you asked –

Wolfgang   What?

Witha   If I'm happy. I am. I've always wanted to live here, ever since the first time they invited us. I just never thought we'd be able to.

Wolfgang   Good.

Witha   What's that face for?

Wolfgang   It smells.

Witha   Of what?

Wolfgang   A Jewish home.

Witha   Have you ever been to a Jewish home?

Wolfgang   This is one.

Witha   Not any more. We'll open a window.

Wolfgang   If it helps.

1978

Heidrun *is pregnant.*

Witha   It smells.

Heidrun   Quiet.

Witha   And the furniture. Depressing.

Heidrun   They can hear you.

Witha   So what? This is my home.

Heidrun   No it's not. It's just that they don't have any money.

Witha   Terrible what they've done to it. How many families live here now?

Heidrun   Three, she said.

Witha   Like stables. This is where your father read from the paper in the morning. I wasn't wearing much yet, and when he glanced over the paper I looked at him so he had to stop reading.

Heidrun Is it all coming back to you now that you're standing here?

Witha You wouldn't think so in this mess, but I can feel your father everywhere. Him coming down the stairs, I feel as if the door is about to open and he'll come in and put his hat on the – but now there's this monster of a mirror. And what have they put in the windows? Are they meant to be curtains?

Heidrun For me everything's gone.

Witha What?

Heidrun If I didn't know I wouldn't realise this was our house. The garden maybe, but it's smaller now.

Witha This is our house underneath all this mildew and junk, I know every stone.

1953

Witha What are you doing?

Heidrun I'm taking the stone.

Witha Look. You've only got the little rucksack. Do you really want to cart a stone over there?

Heidrun Shall I leave it here?

Witha You think they don't have stones in the West?

Heidrun Not this one.

Witha If they search your rucksack at the border and there's a stone, they'll have to start a conversation, why the stone, what do you need it for, are you going to throw it, if there's a stone in your rucksack –

Heidrun Then I'll tell them it's a lucky charm.

Witha   Because you need luck now that you're escaping to the West?

Heidrun   –

Witha   I'm only saying what they're going to say. And the stone hasn't brought us any luck.

Heidrun   I know, but you said it's a special stone because they threw it at Father, you said the stone is a memorial to Father because he financed the Jews' escape, a tiny memorial that you need courage, that Father had courage, and that we must never forget.

Witha   Right. We won't forget, we'll never forget, with or without the stone.

Heidrun   Then I'll leave it here?

Witha *nods.*

Heidrun   And then?

Witha   Look. We'll dig a hole in the garden and put it in there. We'll bury the stone.

Heidrun   Then it's gone.

Witha   No. It'll be there and we'll both know that it's there. And maybe, one day, someone will dig it up again.

1935

A window gets smashed.

Wolfgang   I'm going to tell them off.

Witha   No.

Wolfgang   I'm going to tell them. They're smashing one window after another.

Witha   They'll set fire to the house.

Wolfgang (*shouts*)   It's the wrong house! You're smashing the wrong windows! Leave us alone, we haven't done anything!

1993

Heidrun   Why not ring the doorbell? That would be easier.

Stefanie   But it's not easy. I liked the way you smelled of perfume. I'd never smelled that before.

Heidrun   I'd like to help you, but you really scared us.

Stefanie   Right. A figure behind the window. I wanted to see how you live here. With coffee, outside the winter evening descends early, but there's no snow yet, nature contracts in the cold, but inside you light the lamp over the table and drink real coffee.

Witha   What does she want?

Heidrun   What do you want?

Hannah   She wants to bother us.

Stefanie   You owe me fifteen chocolate bars.

Witha   She's mad.

Stefanie   Fifteen chocolate bars from the West.

Witha (*to* **Hannah**)   Go, child, call the police.

Stefanie   I want my life back.

Heidrun   We haven't got it.

Stefanie   And I want it in chocolate.

Witha (*to* **Hannah**)   Run, child.

Stefanie   Do you know where you are?

Heidrun   This is my home.

Stefanie   You're in my grandfather's home. He's dead now.

Heidrun   I'm sorry, but the house is still –

Stefanie   No, he died because he had to leave this house. Because you thought it was suddenly yours. Where have you been for the past forty years?

Witha   He died, did he?

Stefanie   Yes, didn't know where he was any more, four months, then he was dead. You can't move old people like plants, they shrivel up and die. My grandfather walked into walls at night, peed in the wardrobe, fell down stairs and put his hands through closed windows. In the end he stopped talking, stopped eating, just sat in his chair and stared at his fingers that were moving like a group of people.

Witha   He was over eighty, it's normal to get confused and die.

Stefanie   Oh, really? Then why don't you die too?

Witha   Of course. I fully intend to.

Stefanie   I'm not leaving.

1978

Heidrun *is pregnant.*

Heidrun   Why Heidrun?

Witha   What?

Heidrun   Why did you call me Heidrun?

Witha   No one calls you Heidrun. Everyone says Heidi.

Heidrun   But it says Heidrun in my passport. Because that's the name you gave me. How did you come up with it?

Witha   Don't you like your name?

Heidrun   No.

Witha   Pity.

Heidrun   Heidrun. Sounds like plaited blonde crowns and dirndls.

Witha   You had that and it looked pretty, everyone said so.

Heidrun   I keep thinking, if I have my child now, and it needs a name – it fixes too many things. If I say this is a Petra, then it'll be a Petra, and that's different from saying this is a Beatrix.

Witha   We can call her Beate.

Heidrun   Why did you want me to be a Heidrun?

Witha   I don't think there's anything wrong with it. You turned into a fine Heidrun.

Heidrun   Did you know it's the name of a goat? A mythological goat that produces milk?

Witha   What kind of goat?

Heidrun   A Nordic goat whose milk makes you immortal because it feeds from the tree of life. Was that what you were thinking of – one of those Nordic women with blonde braids that eats leaves and produces good milk?

Witha   Are you upset? Why are you suddenly upset?

Heidrun   Because I don't get it, runes and Nordic and all that. It doesn't fit.

Witha   I just thought about Heidi. I had a friend back then who was called Heidi.

Heidrun   And?

Witha   A pretty, courageous woman. That's what I thought my daughter should be like. I thought it was a pretty name.

Heidrun   Then why didn't you call me Heidi?

Witha   Because that's a child's name and we hoped that at some point you would grow up, and then you'd have a whole name, like a human being.

Heidrun   Heidrun. A Heidrun being. Pretty and courageous. Why was she courageous, this Heidi?

Witha   Heidi?

Heidrun   Yes, this Heidi of yours. Why was she courageous?

Witha   She wasn't afraid, that's all.

Heidrun   Of what?

Witha   Of whatever.

Heidrun   Of the Nazis?

Witha   On the whole. The Nazis, yes.

Heidrun   What did she do to the Nazis?

Witha   I can't remember.

Heidrun   If she was so courageous, what did she do?

Witha   I can't remember, it's a long time ago.

Heidrun   You have to remember something, if she impressed you that much, this Heidi.

Witha   This one time two boys in uniform appeared in her garden.

Heidrun   SS.

Witha   Or Hitler Youth, and she went onto the terrace and shouted at them until they climbed over the fence and left, that's how forceful a woman she was.

Heidrun   And you named me after her?

Witha   Because we wanted you to have some of her strength.

Heidrun   Heidi. But I'm scared. A lot of the time.

Witha   And what are you going to call your child? Petra or – what was the other one?

Heidrun   Daniel if it's a boy. Or Hannah, for a girl. Hannah means grace. No goat, hopefully.

1935

Witha   You can believe me that I find the circumstances under which —

Mieze   Really? Can I believe you?

Witha   That I'm not at all happy about all this.

Mieze   What aren't you happy about?

Witha   All I'm trying to say, is that I feel for you.

Mieze   For me?

Witha   Yes.

Mieze   Do you know how it feels?

Witha   I can imagine.

Mieze   Because the way it feels is irrelevant, the way it feels isn't the problem. That's why it doesn't matter what you imagine.

Witha   It's not our fault that —

Mieze   Who's making you do it?

Witha   You benefit from it as well. Where else are you going to get the money?

Mieze   It's not as if I want to leave.

Witha   No, I know.

Mieze   Exactly. Two suitcases. That's it.

1978

Heidrun *is pregnant.*

Stefanie   My grandad doesn't want to see you.

Heidrun   Aha.

Stefanie   I don't understand, I think he's confused.

Witha   What did he say?

Stefanie   He says you've come about the chickens?

Witha   The chickens.

Stefanie   Yes. I've no idea what he means.

Heidrun   We haven't come about the chickens, I'd just like to see the garden again.

Stefanie   My grandad says no.

Heidrun   No?

Stefanie   He said to send you away because you're only here because of the chickens, but I don't know how I'm meant to send you away.

Witha   We're leaving. It's all right.

Heidrun   No.

Stefanie   I don't even know what chickens he's talking about.

Heidrun   Look. We mean no harm. We used to live here. I'm having a baby. We've come on this trip. That's all I want to see. Just the garden. He doesn't even have to know.

Stefanie   I'm supposed to lie to him?

Heidrun   No. Just don't tell him I was in the garden.

Stefanie   Because I don't want to lie to him. He'll ask.

Heidrun   I'll send you chocolate. Every year. For your birthday.

Stefanie   Like this one?

Heidrun   Yes. Even better ones.

Stefanie   Chocolate.

1945

Wolfgang *is drunk and sitting under the table.*

Witha   I'm taking Heidrun to the basement.

Wolfgang   If I go into the basement the whole house is going to come crashing down.

Witha   It's going to crash down anyway. The town's already on fire.

Wolfgang   And you hide in the basement like a woodlouse. What are you going to tell your daughter?

Witha   You should be glad that she's still alive and has a mother who can still tell her things, because she won't have a father.

Wolfgang   A woodlouse.

Witha   Maybe I'll tell her that – how her father got drunk and sat under the table and waited for his own house to strike him dead, and didn't think about his child for a second.

Wolfgang   At some point you'll climb out of your basement, from the rubble, and everything out there has been blown away, our whole life.

Witha   My life isn't out there, my life is where I am.

Wolfgang   The life of a basement woodlouse. I'm not going to cower any more, if it ends, I can take it.

Witha   It's not going to end.

The light goes out.

The electricity.

Wolfgang   Now the end has begun. Now we can open the window and watch the town burn. Come here.

Witha   Under the table?

Wolfgang   Come. Or the plaster's going to drop on your head.

1993

Heidrun   See that?

Stefanie   What?

Heidrun   Look at the china. My mother's parents lived by the Großer Garten where nothing was left standing on the night of the bombing, they made it to the Südallee, in the park, and then they suffocated from the smoke. The house burned to the ground. But a few days later, when the rubble had cooled off, my mother went back with a handcart and dug the china out of the basement with her bare fingers. (*To* **Witha**.) Isn't that right?

Witha   With my bare fingers.

Heidrun   See that?

Stefanie   What?

Heidrun   The dirt that can't be washed off, this fine grit is burned in, because the glaze melted in the heat from the fire bombs and sealed in the debris. You're eating cake from my grandparents' destroyed house. Now do you understand? With her bare fingers. Do you understand that we belong here?

Stefanie   Because of the china? I don't want any cake. I want chocolate. Fifteen chocolate bars.

1935

Wolfgang *picks up the stone.*

Wolfgang   Why is this still lying around here?

Witha   I thought we could take it to the police and –

Wolfgang   We're not going to the police. We're going to the glazier's.

Witha   You're not going to do anything?

Wolfgang   As long as I've got enough money to afford new glass.

Witha   But if they smash our windows.

Wolfgang   See? They smash our windows and we haven't done anything yet. What do you think they're going to do if we go to the − we won't find a lawyer either. I'm not going to meddle with them. We should never have moved here, into a Jewhouse.

Witha   But the Jews are gone now. They just need to understand that out there.

Wolfgang   Maybe one day they will. Until then, please put the stone away.

Witha   I'll use it as a paperweight on my desk.

1978

Heidrun *is pregnant.*

Stefanie   What is she still doing out there?

Witha   I don't know.

Stefanie   And it's started to rain.

Witha   She likes going for walks in the rain.

Stefanie   But she's not going for a walk.

Witha (*shouts*)   Heidi? Heidi, come in.

Stefanie   She's going to catch cold, and she's having a baby.

Witha   She won't get sick, she's just got silly ideas. (*Shouts.*) Heidrun! What are you doing?

Stefanie   She's kneeling by the bushes.

Witha (*shouts*)   Stop that nonsense. (*To* **Stefanie**.) I know what she's doing.

Stefanie   What?

Witha (*shouts*)   Stop digging. You're not going to find anything.

Stefanie   She's digging?

Witha   Yes. She's digging.

Stefanie   Under our rhododendron?

Witha   She buried something there when she was a child.

Stefanie   Under our bushes?

Witha   Look at her digging.

Stefanie   She's soaking wet. (*Shouts.*) Come inside, you're getting wet.

Witha   Don't bother shouting. She's set her mind on it.

Stefanie   Like a dog digging up a bone.

Heidrun *puts a stone on the table.*

Heidrun   Is this it?

Stefanie   You said you just wanted to stand in the garden.

Heidrun   This is it, right?

Witha   Yes. Whatever.

Heidrun   A stone like from the pavement out front.

Witha   Yes, why not? Then that's the one.

Stefanie   You got dirt all over the lawn.

Heidrun   Come on, let's go.

Stefanie   Wait. I'll fetch you a towel.

Heidrun   Let's get out of here.

Witha   Yes.

Stefanie   But – but I haven't told you when my birthday is yet.

1935

A window gets smashed.

Wolfgang (*jumps to his feet and screams*)   We're not Jewish.
They don't live here any more. We're decent Germans. It's the
wrong house. We're not Jewish.

1935

Nothing.

Mieze   And now we've run out of things to talk about.

Witha   Sorry. I was lost in thought for a moment.

Mieze   What thought?

Witha   Nothing.

Mieze   You looked at the garden.

Witha   I wasn't thinking about the garden.

Mieze   Did you picture yourself welcoming guests on the
veranda and strolling down to the lawn with glasses in your
hands?

Witha   No.

Mieze   Because you can. Over three very shallow steps. I'm
sorry. I'm not a good hostess today.

Witha   Not at all.

Mieze   What?

Witha   I mean no, of course, very good hostess.

Mieze   I'm usually very adept at making conversation.

Witha   I'm sure.

Mieze   It's just taking too long in there.

Witha   Yes, very long, no?

Mieze   Yes, very long.

Nothing

Here we go again.

Witha   What?

Mieze   This silence. It's like a slap in the face.

Witha   I don't mind.

Mieze   Do you think they're silent in there as well?

Witha   I don't know −

Mieze   The longer it takes in there . . . Because I don't think they're silent.

Witha   No?

Mieze   No. Everything was settled long ago, your husband only needed to put his signature at the bottom − three minutes, five, at most. But it's been an hour, and that means your husband hasn't just put his signature − you see, they've started to negotiate in there.

Witha   But isn't that normal?

Mieze   In there your husband is talking to my husband about cracks in the facade and bubbles in the parquet floor and says he won't pay the price because he knows that in the end my husband has to say yes to everything. We're moving out and you're moving in.

Witha   I don't know much about those things.

Mieze   No? But it's not that difficult to understand. Your husband is bringing down the price. Why should he pay for all the furniture if he doesn't even want it?

Witha   Is he meant to? Do you think that would be fair?

Mieze   Do you play the piano?

Witha   You've already asked me that.

Mieze   Maybe you'd like me to play you something, seeing as you're paying for a piano that you have no need for.

1993

Hannah   I'm not staying here.

Heidrun   Where do you want to go?

Hannah   I don't know anyone here. At school they laugh about the way I talk. I'm going to America.

Heidrun   Aren't you a bit young for that?

Hannah   I'm not talking about emigrating. Just for a year, like schoolkids do.

Heidrun   But we've only just got here.

Hannah   Dad says it's a good idea and he's going to pay for me.

Heidrun   But you don't know anyone there.

Hannah   Yes I do. I want to meet the family that Grandad saved. In New York. Mrs Schwarzmann.

Heidrun   Schwarzmann, yes, but what do you want from them?

Hannah   I thought we had a connection.

Heidrun   We do.

Hannah   But I can't feel it here. No one knows about it. At school they scratch swastikas in their desks with their compasses and no one knows who I am. I thought if I go there, if I shake her hand, if Mrs Schwarzmann opens her door to me, I'll feel better.

Heidrun   We can do nice things here as well. We can go to the Elbe Sandstone Mountains. You can take piano lessons. That way you'll meet other children.

Hannah   I don't need other children. You don't want me to leave because you'll be left with your mother. But I don't want to be left with you either.

1993

Witha *is wearing a bridal veil and is digging through a trunk.*

Heidrun   Dear Witha. Today we celebrate yours and Wolfgang's wedding anniversary.

Witha   I'm glad you said that. I was wondering why I'm wearing this white thing.

Heidrun   You met at the AAC, the Academic Athletic Club –

Witha   I know where we met.

Heidrun   Where Father looked after your horse. You must have been quite an impetuous horsewoman.

Hannah   You say that every year.

Heidrun   Your horse needed so much looking after that you had many hours to get to know each other.

Witha   Mmm.

Heidrun   Mother?

Witha   Yes?

Heidrun   This is a speech, and you keep digging through that box.

Witha   I'm looking for the medal.

Heidrun   What medal?

Witha   My medal, the one I got for the War Graves Commission.

Hannah   Her Order of Merit of the Federal Republic of Germany. She's been looking for it all morning.

Witha   I need to wear the medal when it's about Wolfgang. The nice medal with the ribbon.

Heidrun   Have you lost it?

Witha   Did I do the packing or did you? I can't find it. Left behind, stolen.

Heidrun   With your jewellery?

Hannah   We've already looked there.

Heidrun   With your papers, with the letters?

Witha   The letters?

Heidrun   Somewhere among your papers.

Witha   The letters. Wait.

She gets up.

Heidrun   What is it?

Witha   Wait. Now I remember.

She goes towards the garden.

Heidrun   Where are you going?

Witha   In the garden.

Hannah   The Order of Merit? (*To* **Heidrun**.) What does she mean?

Heidrun   No idea. (*To* **Witha**.) Why don't you stay here?

Witha   I buried it. Here in this garden. Don't you remember? We buried it together.

She starts to dig.

Hannah (*to* **Heidrun**)   You buried the Order of Merit in the garden?

Witha   By the rhododendron. Here by the bushes. The beautiful medal.

Heidrun   No. No, you're getting confused.

Hannah   What?

Heidrun   Stop digging, Mother, you're only going to get dirty.

Witha   This is where I buried it. Why don't you help me?

Heidrun (*to* **Witha**)   The pretty veil.

Hannah   Shall I go and fetch her?

Heidrun   She's set her mind on it.

Hannah   But what is she doing?

Heidrun   She won't find anything. Let's have a toast. You can have a sip as well. Cheers.

Hannah   Aha. Cheers.

1945 / 1953

Witha *takes a letter from the box and reads it.*

Wolfgang   The Führer is dead and Germany lies in ruins. I suppose it's all coming to an end. I was going to do it in my office, the place where I fulfilled my duty as head of the Institute. It would have been a heroic gesture and would have lifted the burden off your shoulders, dear Witha. But now that my office has burned to cinders with all the rest I have to do it at home. It breaks my heart, my dear, that you will find me like this. But I'm afraid I can't spare you. None of us are spared. Tell our little daughter, when she's old enough, that I died as an upright German. Maybe she'll take comfort from that. The most painful thought is that I'm leaving you both behind. But it's the fate of war that the men die and the women stay behind. Now it's your fate too, because I can't take you with me. Bear it with proud dignity and in the consciousness –

Witha   'And in the consciousness' has been crossed out.

Wolfgang   Bear it with proud dignity, just as I preserve my dignity as a German officer by taking this final step.

Witha   'Of a German officer' is crossed out.

Wolfgang   God bless –

Witha   'God bless' is crossed out as well.

Wolfgang   Heil Hitler.

Nothing. **Witha** *looks at the sheet of paper, then she slowly tears it to pieces.*

1953

Heidrun   Everyone said their fathers were killed in Russia or on the Western Front, or missing and things like that, so I had to say something too. Russia, I said, but I don't actually know.

Witha   No, he didn't fight in the war, horses were vital to the war effort, that's why they didn't send vets to the front. Not when they were in charge of an institute vital to the war effort.

Heidrun   Then why did he die? Or didn't he?

Witha   He did. When the Russians marched in, he was standing upstairs by the window.

Heidrun   Cheering.

Witha   What?

Heidrun   Cheering on the Russians.

Witha   The Russians?

Heidrun   Because they freed the city. Freed Germany from the Nazis.

Witha   Exactly. Everyone was standing by the windows. I put a white towel out and he said don't take such an old rag, take a good one.

Heidrun   In order to show respect for the Red Army.

Witha   Exactly. And then they went past and we were looking down to see if we could make out the faces of the Mongolians, because everyone knew the Mongolians are ruthless, and they kept lifting their rifles to shoot celebratory shots, and suddenly your father sinks down and his blood runs over the white towel, and it was a head shot. From a Russian who wasn't looking, who shot him with a celebratory shot just when the war had ended.

1993

Heidrun   So don't think that you're the only ones that suffered under socialism. We've paid our dues.

Stefanie   I didn't know that, but what does that –

Heidrun (*interrupts her*)   Because it's not something you write on a banner and put in the window.

Hannah   And it's a tragedy that he, just when it was actually over – with a celebratory shot. And that the Russians got the wrong man, because he was on their side, it was completely wrong that he had to die.

Heidrun   It's all right, Hannah, I'll take care of this. (*To* **Stefanie**.) You want to talk about the house?

Stefanie   About the house, yes.

Heidrun   The mortar is falling off the facade.

Stefanie   We didn't have enough money to replaster the facade for you, sorry, but you're rich, you can put up a new facade.

Heidrun   That's not what this is about.

Stefanie   Of course, for the masonry it's better, if that's what you mean, a few more years and you wouldn't have had to wait for the system to collapse, the whole country would have collapsed, literally, the buildings, caved in one after the other, the whole country caved in, irretrievably, if that's what you were trying to say.

Heidrun   The mortar. If you wash the paint off the façade, or if you just run your hand over it hard a couple of times when everything is wet from the rain, then you've got red-colour particles on your hand. Red. Do you think the house was painted red once?

Stefanie   The house has always been white.

Heidrun   Exactly. Yet there's red. I'm not lying to you. Of course the house has always been white. But in the thirties some men came with paint and paintbrushes and painted on the facade in red. Did you know that?

Stefanie   What kind of men?

Heidrun   My father financed a Jewish family, financed their escape, gave them money so they could emigrate. And that's why they painted insults on the facade. At first he kept painting over it, with white, in the end he bore their scribbles with pride, like a medal. You didn't know that, did you?

Stefanie   No.

Heidrun   And here –

She places the stone on the table.

The fact that you're not calling attention to yourself doesn't mean you've got something to hide. This is no ordinary stone.

Stefanie   Cobblestone.

Heidrun   They threw this stone at my father because he gave the Jewish family money. But he bent down and picked the stone up and put it in his pocket. And now the stone is lying on this table.

Stefanie   You dug it out of my garden. Is that the one? From my rhododendron.

Heidrun   What I'm trying to say is: this is not your garden. It never was. This is my father's house, he fought a lonely battle here, he put the spikes on the garden wall to protect his family from the Nazis, he lived with the humiliations and the danger but they didn't manage to break him, he had stones thrown at him and in the end he was shot up there, in the room that maybe was your nursery for a few years. There weren't many people like my father, people who proved that resistance was possible, people who risked their lives for others. My father was one of those exceptions and yet no one knows his story. You – you lived here for a while, in his house, fine, you didn't pay a penny in rent all those years since we had to leave the country, and we never complained. But now you stand in his garden, sit at our table, in all your youthful ignorance and impudence, and talk about a place you obviously know nothing about – aren't you ashamed of yourself?

Stefanie   What?

Heidrun   If you're not ashamed of yourself –

Witha   Hannah? Why is your mother getting so upset?

Stefanie   How was I supposed to know? You were gone. You never sent any chocolate. My grandfather died. I just wanted to come home.

Heidrun   Exactly. You can have a coffee and then you're leaving.

Stefanie   To go where?

Heidrun   Home.

Stefanie   I thought that was here.

Heidrun   No. You've already moved out. This place is occupied. You didn't realise, but the house was always inhabited. The whole time. From the room where my father died down to the basement where my mother survived the bombing. You were only visiting. And that's why you have to go home now.

1993

Stefanie   My grandfather told me it was an accident, tried to explain it to me. That they were travelling in the car, my parents, at night in the rain towards Plauen, and they went off the road and into a tree. I didn't like the forest after that, kept swinging towards the house, the trees were too creepy. Then I heard about the Flight from the Republic for the first time, heard about it at school, how people escape to the West and leave everything. I knew at once that my parents aren't dead, that they left me, their car didn't smash into a tree, it's standing in a garage in the West, and I kept wondering is it in Frankfurt or in Hamburg, we sometimes got parcels from there, from relatives I didn't know, from the West, for Christmas. I never told my grandad about it and never asked, and I always loved him for wanting to protect me from the truth. Now he's dead and I've started looking, in the West, for my parents. But there's no one with that name. Not in Frankfurt, not in Hamburg, not anywhere. Maybe my father died in the meantime and my mother remarried and has a different name. They're gone. I'm alone now.

1993

Heidrun   Do you recognise it?

Witha   What?

Hannah   The house.

Witha   What house?

Heidrun   This is where we live now. Like before.

Witha   Here? No, I live somewhere else.

Heidrun   You can have the room at the top, with a view of the garden.

Witha   And how am I supposed to get up the stairs?

Heidrun   Or you can have the garden room down here.

Witha   And when are we going back home?

Heidrun   We're staying here.

Hannah   She doesn't recognise it.

Heidrun   This is our house. Your house. This is where you lived with Father. With Wolfgang.

Witha   I know what your father's name is. But they've cleared everything away. We should have kept the furniture after all.

Heidrun   What furniture?

Witha   The piano stood here.

Heidrun   No. There was no piano. You're getting confused.

Witha   No. I'm not getting confused. Here. The piano.

Heidrun   But you've never played the piano.

Witha   I didn't. But Mieze did.

Hannah   Mieze?

Heidrun   That's her friend from back then.

Witha   Mieze played the piano beautifully.

1935

Mieze *returns with an axe.*

Mieze   You wanted some music for your ears?

Witha   Mrs Schwarzmann?

Mieze   No, no, don't worry, it's just an axe. The gardener uses it when he needs to chop something, since there are trees on the property.

Witha   But what do you need it for?

Mieze   It's almost a little forest. Hear that?

Witha   What?

Mieze   The rustling from the garden. It's the wind in the branches.

Witha   I think I'd better fetch my husband.

Mieze   No, let's not bother the men, I'm sure they're almost done and your husband is just saying we'll deduct the piano, we don't need it.

Witha   Is that what he's saying?

Mieze   Or you can reconsider and take lessons. You'll be able to play 'Frère Jacques' in no time.

Witha   I'm not going to take lessons.

Mieze   It's called 'Bruder Jakob' now. No? You don't want to? 'Bruder Jakob'. I'll show you.

Witha   Take it with you, your piano, if you're so obsessed with it, I don't want it.

Mieze   So you got angry after all, even though I've got an axe in my hand.

Witha   And it makes no sense that we should have to pay for it if we don't need it.

Mieze   Hence the axe.

Witha   What?

Mieze   I'm taking it with me, the piano. If you won't pay for it you're not going to get it. I'll play you a goodbye song. Listen carefully. It's the last time someone's going to play on it.

She goes and chops up the piano.

1993

Hannah   Can you help me?

Witha   What is it, child?

Hannah   I want to write a letter.

Witha   To whom?

Hannah   Actually, I want you to write a letter.

Witha   Oh, really?

Hannah   Yes, for me.

Witha   Why don't you write the letter yourself?

Hannah   I don't know the person.

Witha   Why do you want to write to someone you don't even know?

Hannah   Mrs Schwarzmann. Mrs Schwarzmann in New York.

Witha   Schwarzmann.

Hannah   Yes.

Witha   I knew them.

Hannah   So will you write the letter for me?

Witha   But that's not possible, child.

Hannah   Please. I want to visit them when I'm in America, there are so many things I want to ask her.

Witha   But you can't, child.

Hannah   I've found her address. In Brooklyn. She's called Shwartzman now. It's spelled differently but it's got to be her. Deborah Shwartzman.

Witha   Her name isn't Deborah. Her name is Mieze.

Hannah   Mieze is not a name.

Witha   Yes it is. Mieze. Mignon. Mieze.

Hannah   Mignon?

Witha   It's supposed to be French. Sounds funny. That's why she's called Mieze.

Hannah   But Mignon, is that a Jewish name?

Witha   No. Her husband didn't have sidelocks either, and he treated pigs.

Hannah   Then maybe it's her daughter.

Witha   No.

Hannah   How would you know?

Witha   She's dead. She doesn't have a daughter. She never made it to America, child.

Hannah   Yes she did. She was in Amsterdam. She met Max Beckmann. She took his paintings from the frames and sewed them into the lining of her suitcase. She brought him to America.

Witha   Is that right? I think I read that somewhere.

Hannah   Because it happened.

Witha   But not because of her. I don't think the Schwarzmanns ever went to Amsterdam. They were picked up, like all the others.

Hannah   You saved them.

Witha   Yes? I thought someone told the SA.

Hannah   Who?

Witha   I think someone reported them for saying something and they were arrested out there, by the front door, with their suitcases, and taken away.

Hannah   Someone.

Witha   Yes, child.

Hannah   No.

Witha   Yes.

1935

Mieze   Mrs Heising, would you like to be my friend?

Witha   But I already am.

Mieze   No, would you like to be my friend? We've known each other for such a long time, how long?

Witha   I don't know, one, two –

Mieze   Longer, the dinner parties when my husband was still running the Institute, it must be more than three years, and out of all those people you're the only one who still comes to visit.

Witha   Yes.

Mieze   Evil tongues might say you only came to take the house away from us, but we're not evil, are we?

Witha   Of course not, what do you mean – 'evil'?

Mieze   I want to be your friend, it doesn't matter now anyway, tomorrow we're gone, I'm Mieze.

Witha   I don't know if that's possible.

Mieze   When we're in a foreign county it would be so nice to know that there are friends living in our house. Sorry.

Witha   What?

Mieze   It would be yours. You'd be living in your house, not in ours, you would have bought it, you're buying it as we speak, I'm Mieze, don't you want to tell me your name?

Witha   We shouldn't do this without our husbands, I think –

Mieze   No, because, you know, when our husbands walk out of that door it might already be much more difficult to be friends with you. I know your name is Roswitha, can I call you Witha? Our husbands will never know, tomorrow I'm gone, we'll have a toast with cups of coffee, Witha, may I? There won't be any more embarrassing meetings, you'll never see me again, it's just for tonight, so I know that you'll never forget me, that you won't forget your friend Mieze.